9 Dangerous Ideas - Area 51 and Extra-Terrestrials

By Ratzinger

Copyright © 2015

www.9DangerousIdeas.com

9 DANGEROUS
IDEAS

Weapons Of Mass Distraction They Use To Steal Your Freedom...

Ratzinger

Welcome To 9 Dangerous Ideas...

The existence of a group that is "stage-managing" the world may be frightening, but sometimes it's not hard to accept. It could be argued that we accept it already, in a way, but simply aren't aware of our acceptance. How often do we find ourselves saying things like, "They should do something about world hunger," or "They're letting too many Third World countries default on their debts," or "They're letting inflation get out of control?"

We live in an information age – or maybe more accurately an attention age. You probably feel like we're not being told the truth, leaving us instead to be the working cattle that keep society ticking over. And you probably suspect that the powers that be deliberately engineer world changing events for their own power and gain, costing us our freedom, health and civil rights.

The truth is you have no idea how to change it or beat the puppet masters. If you did then you'd be doing it.

Like me, your aim is probably to determine the facts and uncover the truth, wake up more people and let them make up their own minds, because deep down you truly value your freedom and having a bright future for your kids. But you're absolutely terrified that some sceptic will pick holes in your argument and you'll have nothing to answer with.

Isn't it frustrating when you're not believed, not being taken seriously, being thought of as a crackpot? The agenda being pushed forward and you're trying to raise awareness, wake people up, standing up for what you believe in.

What needs to happen? **For more people to look into conspiracy theories and question authority.** There's been an explosion of web sites, blogs and videos on different topics like the New World order, 911 investigation, moon landing hoaxes, etc. Yet trying to convince other people that you're right, or that they should at least look into it, often falls on deaf ears... or gets you laughed at.

If you're like me, you've always wanted to get people to listen to you, and get them to see that they're being lied to every day and they're not really free. But there's a nagging doubt inside that wonders if you know enough about conspiracy theories to be taken seriously. So you surf the web looking for moon landing hoaxes, conspiracy theories and info on the Freemasons...

Or you keep up to date with David Icke, Alex Jones' Infowars...

But don't you just hate it when you have to argue with friends, family and colleagues who don't believe you? How much more money do you have to spend on books and DVDs before the penny drops?

I always thought *"if only someone could show me a fair summary of both sides of the argument so I can make up my own mind"*. Then I realise that yet again, I forgot to do my own research before jumping on the next explanation...

My Story...

I grew up a good catholic boy, loving space stuff – I had my own telescope, loved sci-fi, the space shuttle, NASA. But have you ever noticed that all the big events happen in, or are connected to, The United States of America? Obviously being one of the major superpowers, the USA has great influence on the planet. Being outside the USA we can see things more objectively though, as we're not subjected to the same level of conditioning and patriotism. Some would call it brainwashing...

There's a guy in my street who is a Freemason. I was always curious about the secret society that was allegedly started by the Vatican. Pope John Paul was shot in 1981 and there was a story about him throwing up a Freemason symbol for help. When I broached the subject with my neighbour he was taken aback at first, but then got quite excited at my curiosity...

 See I was at a relative's house when 911 was shown on the news. I was still at primary school, but even though I was young, I thought to myself "Something doesn't feel right..." Here's another thing – the Sixteenth century French writer Nostradamus is thought to have predicted that the two tallest buildings would fall...

"Two steel birds will fall from the sky on the Metropolis / The sky will burn at forty-five degrees latitude / Fire approaches the great new city / Immediately a huge, scattered flame leaps up / Within months, rivers will flow with blood / The undead will roam the earth for little time."

Everyone else bought into the Bin Laden explanation but my uncle and I didn't buy it. We discussed it amongst ourselves, but didn't really mention our theories to anyone else in case they thought we were a bit weird. Maybe you can relate? We discussed it amongst ourselves and felt almost guilty for questioning it. Those buildings certainly looked like they were brought down by controlled demolition. Do you remember the BBC newscaster who reported the destruction of Building 7... BEFORE the building fell? And if a plane really did hit the Pentagon, why was all the CCTV footage confiscated? Why wouldn't they just let us see the actual aircraft hitting the actual building. The 911 events featured 4 different aircraft, but no wreckage, no black boxes... So I started looking into it on YouTube, and other internet sites, where I watched videos about Bohemian Grove with all the world's leaders present. Then I realised the implications of it all...

Have you ever seen weird lights in the sky? I have... in the skies above Scotland. Three years ago I saw a red orb in the sky at night while out with a mate. It moved in a strange way for a good five minutes. Honestly I was so scared, cos I couldn't tell what it was. I kept that to myself as well and we never talked about it ever again. Yes I've seen weird lights in the skies above Scotland. In fact one local area nearby is renowned for UFO sightings. There have been too many abductions, crop circles and mutilated cattle to think it's all just random or isolated incidents.

The base's current primary purpose is publicly unknown; however, based on historical evidence, it most likely supports development and testing of experimental aircraft and weapons systems (black projects). The intense secrecy surrounding the base has made it the frequent subject of conspiracy theories and a central component to unidentified flying object (UFO) folklore. Although the base has never been declared a secret base, all research and occurrences in Area 51 are Top Secret/Sensitive Compartmented Information. In July 2013, following a FOIA request filed in 2005, the CIA publicly acknowledged the existence of the base for the first time, declassifying documents detailing the history and purpose of Area 51.

In 2012 my mate and I saw red orbs in the sky that move in extraordinary ways, and silently. We were so scared we told no one, keeping it to ourselves and never discussing it again. People would think we were bonkers! But I grew up fascinated with space, science fiction, telescopes. Having witnessed these unidentified flying objects first hand, you can understand my curiosity around the subject. Have you ever seen something in the sky that you couldn't identify? Once you've had a "Close Encounter", there's no going back. I mean, have you ever wondered if there's life elsewhere?

In **ufology**, a close encounter is an event in which a person witnesses an unidentified flying object. This terminology and the system of classification behind it was started by astronomer and UFO researcher J. Allen Hynek, and was first suggested in his 1972 book The UFO Experience: A Scientific Inquiry. He introduced the first three kinds of encounters; more sub-types of close encounters were later added by others, but these additional categories are not universally accepted by UFO researchers, mainly because they depart from the scientific rigor that Hynek aimed to bring to ufology

Close Encounters of the First kind

Visual sightings of an unidentified flying object seemingly less than 500 feet away that show an appreciable angular extension and considerable detail. Like silent spheres over parts of Scotland.

Close Encounters of the Second kind

A UFO event in which a physical effect is alleged. This can be interference in the functioning of a vehicle or electronic device; animals reacting; a physiological effect such as paralysis or heat and discomfort in the witness; or some physical trace like impressions in the ground, scorched or otherwise affected vegetation, or a chemical trace. We've all seen pictures of crop circles, mutilated cattle, or abductees suffering strange burns or scratches.

Cattle mutilations, radiation around the carcass, flesh flayed from the bone, or eyes removed, or kidneys surgically extracted. Extra-terrestrial evidence, or the work of a VERY terrestrial nutcase?

Close Encounters of the Third kind

I used to discuss the moon landings with my Dad, and he didn't believe the official line. He'd been a soldier in the Army, and he told me to research it for myself so I did. That sparked the usual questions - why were there no visible stars in the sky above the moon, why was the flag waving, why were there astronaut footprints but no tyre tracks from the moon rover?

See, I grew up a good Catholic boy, but since the Pope John Paul shooting I never trusted him again because there were too many Freemason signs.

You know the kind of signs – you can see Hollywood actors and celebrities showing esoteric symbols and carrying out black magic rituals on stage, dressed up as "performances". Disney friendly Hannah Montana turning into twerking Miley Cyrus. Britney going from sassy schoolgirl to skinhead meltdown. Talk about falling from grace! Kitten programming.

How many celebrities have died under mysterious circumstances: John F. Kennedy, John F. Kennedy Junior, Robert F. Kennedy, Martin Luther King, Michael Jackson, Whitney Houston, Whitney's daughter, Paul Walker, Robin Williams, Bruce Lee, his son Brandon Lee, Marilyn Monroe, Heath Ledger, Princess Diana, Tupac Shakur, John Lennon, Kurt Cobain, Malcolm X. The list goes on and on…

I've been to places where Satanists have carved the trees and sacrificed small animals. I've also been arrested for breach of the peace, and had the Police at my door. I have spoken at length to an old friend who started off certain that the moon landings happened as reported, but now he's changed his mind. And I'm hoping you'll fully consider these "Dangerous Ideas" and maybe think twice…

Growing up I never found anyone to really discuss it with. My friends thought I was bonkers. And it does sound kind of crazy: The mainstream is controlled and feed the public only certain information that they want us to know.

BUT rather than being some evangelistic preacher who tries to convince you, I want to give you both sides of the argument and let you make an informed decision. There's no going back. You can't ignore the signs, there are too many inconsistencies. My goal now is to share these alleged conspiracies with other people and let them decide themselves. Stand up and be counted. We can bring them down. The 85% majority can topple the world elite. The truth is out there…

I know what you're thinking...

I can predict some of the thoughts that have already gone through your mind:

This will be the same old stuff regurgitated – yes there are lots of videos, books, documentaries and websites, and yes I'm acting as a kind of "human Google". <u>I've done all the research so you don't have to.</u> Secondly, I'll repeat that because I reside outside the USA, I have a more objective viewpoint, PLUS I'm also presenting **both sides** of the argument – here's what the conspiracy theorists believe, and here's what the mainstream media would have you believe.

Secondly, you don't know me from Adam, so what gives me the right? Fair point. You don't know me, yet, and that's because you haven't read this entire chapter all the way to the end... yet. But when you do, you'll hopefully understand my story, and appreciate that I've been jailed for my beliefs, I've been surrounded by a Police SWAT team, and I've spoken to the Ministry Of Defence. By the way, that's why I'm keeping my identity secret - to protect myself. I'm not stupid!

This guy's a Crackpot! – I can understand you jumping to that conclusion. But in all honesty, all I'm asking is that you take a look yourself. Are you really that closed minded? Any fair court of law [I should know, I've been in a few!] looks at <u>both sides of the debate.</u> Any mature adult will consider both sides of an argument. Are you only accepting one opinion? Are you actually scared that you might come across something that makes you doubt? And what would happen if you did?

This is an invitation to you to open your mind, become more aware, and wake up to the possibility that we are being manipulated and controlled. Question authority, pull the wool from your eyes and let's see if we can prevent our future children from living in a microchipped hell on earth...

Area 51 and Extra-Terrestrials

You're bound to have heard of Area 51 – actually a remote part of Edwards Air Force Base in the Nevada desert, USA. This monumental location was featured in the movies Independence Day, Indiana Jones, and the Stargate TV series, but it is very real.

If you were to Google Area 51 right now, you'll see the usual photographs, conspiracy theory videos and episodes of The X-Files. There are books, articles, videos on the web. There are also lots of stories of ex-employees who have seen glimpses of aliens, and spacecraft. But once you start to dig a little deeper, which is what I've already done for you, dear reader...

Area 51 is located in the southern portion of Nevada in the western United States, 83 miles (134 km) north-northwest of Las Vegas. Situated at its centre, on the southern shore of Groom Lake, is a large military airfield. The site was acquired by the United States Air Force in 1955, primarily for the flight testing of the super-secret Lockheed U-2 aircraft. The area around Area 51, including the small town of Rachel on the aptly named "Extra-terrestrial Highway", is a popular tourist destination.

The United States Air Force facility commonly known as Area 51 is a remote detachment of Edwards Air Force Base, within the Nevada Test and Training Range. According to the Central Intelligence Agency (CIA), the correct names for the facility are Homey Airport and Groom Lake. Other names used for the facility include Dreamland, and nicknames Paradise Ranch, Home Base and Watertown. The special use airspace around the field is referred to as a Restricted Area 4808 North.

The name "Area 51 "supposedly comes from 1950's Nevada Test site maps. The origin of the Area 51 name isn't totally clear. The most accepted explanation comes from a grid numbering system of the area by the Atomic Energy Commission (AEC); while Area 51 isn't part of this system, it is adjacent to Area 15. Another explanation is that 51 was used because it was unlikely that the AEC would ever use the number.

It's also referred to as Groom Lake, built around Paradise Ranch which was so names to entice employees to work in such a remote location. Named Dreamland after the Edgar Allen Poe poem:

> By a route obscure and lonely,
> Haunted by ill angels only,
> Where an Eidolon, named NIGHT,
> On a black throne reigns upright,
> I have reached these lands but newly

From an ultimate dim Thule—
From a wild weird clime that lieth, sublime,
Out of SPACE—Out of TIME.

Bottomless vales and boundless floods,
And chasms, and caves, and Titan woods,
With forms that no man can discover
For the tears that drip all over;
Mountains toppling evermore
Into seas without a shore;
Seas that restlessly aspire,
Surging, unto skies of fire;
Lakes that endlessly outspread
Their lone waters—lone and dead,—
Their still waters—still and chilly
With the snows of the lolling lily.

By the lakes that thus outspread
Their lone waters, lone and dead,—
Their sad waters, sad and chilly
With the snows of the lolling lily,—
By the mountains—near the river
Murmuring lowly, murmuring ever,—
By the grey woods,—by the swamp
Where the toad and the newt encamp,—
By the dismal tarns and pools
Where dwell the Ghouls,—
By each spot the most unholy—
In each nook most melancholy,—
There the traveller meets, aghast,
Sheeted Memories of the Past—
Shrouded forms that start and sigh
As they pass the wanderer by—
White-robed forms of friends long given,
In agony, to the Earth—and Heaven.

For the heart whose woes are legion
'T is a peaceful, soothing region—
For the spirit that walks in shadow
'T is—oh, 't is an Eldorado!
But the traveller, travelling through it,
May not—dare not openly view it;
Never its mysteries are exposed
To the weak human eye unclosed;
So wills its King, who hath forbid
The uplifting of the fring'd lid;
And thus the sad Soul that here passes
Beholds it but through darkened glasses.

By a route obscure and lonely,
Haunted by ill angels only,

Where an Eidolon, named NIGHT,
On a black throne reigns upright,
I have wandered home but newly
From this ultimate dim Thule.

Source: *The Complete Poems and Stories of Edgar Allan Poe* (1946)

The base's current primary purpose is publicly unknown; however, based on historical evidence, it most likely supports development and testing of experimental aircraft and weapons systems (black projects). The intense secrecy surrounding the base has made it the frequent subject of conspiracy theories and a central component to unidentified flying object (UFO) folklore. Although the base has never been declared a secret base, all research and occurrences in Area 51 are Top Secret/Sensitive Compartmented Information. In July 2013, following a FOIA request filed in 2005, the CIA publicly acknowledged the existence of the base for the first time, declassifying documents detailing the history and purpose of Area 51.

In 2012 my mate and I saw red orbs in the sky that move in extraordinary ways, and silently. We were so scared we told no one, keeping it to ourselves and never discussing it again. People would think we were bonkers! But I grew up fascinated with space, science fiction, telescopes. Having witnessed these unidentified flying objects first hand, you can understand my curiosity around the subject. Have you ever seen something in the sky that you couldn't identify? Once you've had a "Close Encounter", there's no going back. I mean, have you ever wondered if there's life elsewhere?

In **ufology**, a close encounter is an event in which a person witnesses an unidentified flying object. This terminology and the system of classification behind it was started by astronomer and UFO researcher J. Allen Hynek, and was first suggested in his 1972 book The UFO Experience: A Scientific Inquiry. He introduced the first three kinds of encounters; more sub-types of close encounters were later added by others, but these additional categories are not universally accepted by UFO researchers, mainly because they depart from the scientific rigor that Hynek aimed to bring to ufology

Close Encounters of the First kind

Visual sightings of an unidentified flying object seemingly less than 500 feet away that show an appreciable angular extension and considerable detail. Like silent spheres over parts of Scotland.

Close Encounters of the Second kind

A UFO event in which a physical effect is alleged. This can be interference in the functioning of a vehicle or electronic device; animals reacting; a physiological effect such as paralysis or heat and discomfort in the witness; or some physical trace like impressions in the ground, scorched or otherwise affected vegetation, or a chemical trace. We've all seen pictures of crop circles, mutilated cattle, or abductees suffering strange burns or scratches.

Cattle mutilations, radiation around the carcass, flesh flayed from the bone, or eyes removed, or kidneys surgically extracted. Extra-terrestrial evidence, or the work of a VERY terrestrial nutcase?

Close Encounters of the Third kind

UFO encounters in which an animated creature is present. These include humanoids, robots, and humans who seem to be occupants or pilots of a UFO. Steven Spielberg gave us those.

Close Encounters of the Fourth kind

A UFO event in which a human is abducted by a UFO or its occupants. This type was not included in Hynek's original close encounters scale.

Hynek's one-time associate Jacques Vallee argued in the Journal of Scientific Exploration that a CE4 should be described as *"cases when witnesses experienced a transformation of their sense of reality"*, so as to also include non-abduction cases where absurd, hallucinatory or dreamlike events are associated with UFO encounters.

Close Encounters of the Fifth kind

A UFO event that involves direct communication between aliens and humans. This type of close encounter was named by Steven M. Greer's CSETI group and is described as bilateral contact experiences through conscious, voluntary and proactive human-initiated cooperative communication with extra-terrestrial intelligence.

Close Encounters of the Sixth kind

Death of a human or animal associated with a UFO sighting, although some might consider this as a more severe example of a second-kind encounter.

Close Encounters of the Seventh kind
The creation of a human/alien hybrid, either by sexual reproduction or by artificial scientific methods

So what has Area 51 got to do with all this "Close Encounters" malarkey? Well, read on, we're getting to that...

The Groom Lake test facility was established in April 1955 by the Central Intelligence Agency (CIA) for Project Aquatone, the development of the Lockheed U-2 strategic reconnaissance aircraft.

Given the extreme secrecy enveloping the project, the flight test and pilot training programmes could not be conducted at Edwards Air Force Base or Lockheed's Palmdale facility. A search for a suitable testing site for the U-2 was conducted under the same extreme security as the rest of the project. The Director notified Lockheed, who sent an inspection team out to Groom Lake. According to Lockheed's U-2 designer Kelly Johnson:

"... We flew over it and within thirty seconds, you knew that was the place ... it was right by a dry lake. Man alive, we looked at that lake, and we all looked at each other. It was another Edwards, so

UFO encounters in which an animated creature is present. These include humanoids, robots, and humans who seem to be occupants or pilots of a UFO. Steven Spielberg gave us those.

Close Encounters of the Fourth kind

A UFO event in which a human is abducted by a UFO or its occupants. This type was not included in Hynek's original close encounters scale.

Hynek's one-time associate Jacques Vallee argued in the Journal of Scientific Exploration that a CE4 should be described as *"cases when witnesses experienced a transformation of their sense of reality"*, so as to also include non-abduction cases where absurd, hallucinatory or dreamlike events are associated with UFO encounters.

Close Encounters of the Fifth kind

A UFO event that involves direct communication between aliens and humans. This type of close encounter was named by Steven M. Greer's CSETI group and is described as bilateral contact experiences through conscious, voluntary and proactive human-initiated cooperative communication with extra-terrestrial intelligence.

Close Encounters of the Sixth kind

Death of a human or animal associated with a UFO sighting, although some might consider this as a more severe example of a second-kind encounter.

Close Encounters of the Seventh kind
The creation of a human/alien hybrid, either by sexual reproduction or by artificial scientific methods

So what has Area 51 got to do with all this "Close Encounters" malarkey? Well, read on, we're getting to that...

The Groom Lake test facility was established in April 1955 by the Central Intelligence Agency (CIA) for Project Aquatone, the development of the Lockheed U-2 strategic reconnaissance aircraft.

Given the extreme secrecy enveloping the project, the flight test and pilot training programmes could not be conducted at Edwards Air Force Base or Lockheed's Palmdale facility. A search for a suitable testing site for the U-2 was conducted under the same extreme security as the rest of the project. The Director notified Lockheed, who sent an inspection team out to Groom Lake. According to Lockheed's U-2 designer Kelly Johnson:

"... We flew over it and within thirty seconds, you knew that was the place ... it was right by a dry lake. Man alive, we looked at that lake, and we all looked at each other. It was another Edwards, so

we wheeled around, landed on that lake, taxied up to one end of it. It was a perfect natural landing field ... as smooth as a billiard table without anything being done to it". Johnson used a compass to lay out the direction of the first runway. The place was called "Groom Lake".

The lake bed made an ideal strip from which they could test aircraft, and the Emigrant Valley's mountain ranges and the NTS perimeter, about 100 miles north of Las Vegas, protected the test site from visitors. The CIA asked the AEC to acquire the land, designated "Area 51" on the map, and add it to the Nevada Test Site.

They named the area "Paradise Ranch" to encourage workers to move to a place that the CIA's official history of the U-2 project would later describe as "the new facility in the middle of nowhere"; the name became shortened to "the Ranch". On 4 May 1955, a survey team arrived at Groom Lake and laid out a 5,000-foot (1,500 m), north-south runway on the southwest corner of the lakebed and designated a site for a base support facility. By July 1955, CIA, Air Force, and Lockheed personnel began arriving.

SR-71

During the 1960's this was where the first Drones were tested and developed. Later on Lockheed would develop the iconic SR-71 Blackbird here – the fastest and most memorable spy plane in history. In the seventies and eighties they developed the F-117 Stealth fighter here. To maintain top secrecy these were flown to and from the base under cover of darkness.

Since the F-117 became operational in 1983, operations at Groom Lake have continued. The base and its associated runway system were expanded, including expansion of housing and support facilities. In 1995, the federal government expanded the exclusion zone around the base to include nearby mountains that had afforded the only decent overlook of the base. The area surrounding the lake is permanently off-limits both to civilian and normal military air traffic. Security clearances are checked regularly; cameras and weaponry are not allowed. Even military pilots training in the NAFR risk disciplinary action if they stray into the exclusionary "box" surrounding Groom's airspace. Surveillance is supplemented using buried motion sensors.

When documents about the installation become declassified, much of the detail has been deleted. In 1994 five unnamed civilians and two widows sued the USAF on the grounds that chemicals were leaked out of the base and these chemicals directly led to respiratory, liver and skin complaints in the five and the two dead husbands. They demanded information about these chemicals to aid in their treatment, but no information was released on the grounds that it would threaten national security. When judges pressed further, President Bill Clinton stepped in and overruled them, keeping the information classified. The case therefore was dropped due to lack of evidence. An appeal accused the government of abusing its power. The appeal was rejected on the bases that disclosures of the materials present in the air and water near Groom can reveal military operational capabilities or the nature and scope of classified operations.

In 1974 Astronauts aboard Skylab 4 inadvertently took photographs of Area 51. The response by the US government clearly showed that it thought this location was the most "sensitive" place on earth.

Because of this secretive nature and proven connection to classified aircraft projects, together with reports of flying saucer phenomena, Area 51 has become a focus of modern UFO and conspiracy theories. Some of the activities mentioned in such theories at Area 51 include:

The storage, research, and reverse engineering of crashed alien spacecraft (including material supposedly recovered at the Roswell incident), the study of their occupants (allegedly living and dead), and the manufacture of aircraft based on alien technology
Meetings or joint alliances with extra-terrestrial beings.
The development of advanced energy weapons for the Strategic Defence Initiative [The so-called Star Wars programme to shoot ICBM's out of the sky with lasers]
The development of weather control technology
The development of time travel and teleportation technology
The development of unusual and exotic propulsion systems
Activities related to a supposed shadowy Majestic 12 organization

Other theories include claims of a transcontinental Underground Railroad system, a disappearing airstrip (nicknamed the "Cheshire Airstrip", after Lewis Carroll's Cheshire cat) which briefly appears when water is sprayed onto its camouflaged asphalt, and aircraft based on alien technology.

Several ex-employees have revealed details about the base – Bob Lazar mentioned an underground level where he worked with others on alien craft that the US government had in its possession. In the 1950's Bruce Burgess claimed he had worked on a flying disc simulator, based on the design of the crashed craft they stored there. He also mentioned an alien translator called J-Rod who was telepathic. In 2004 Dan Burisch claimed to have worked alongside J-Rod, while developing alien viruses. Ebola anyone?

In any case, this is the most secure military base in the world – protected by cameras and military personnel, including the use of deadly force. Some believe it's a nuclear testing site. Others have witnessed strange aircraft taking off silently then accelerating at unearthly speed into the night sky, defying gravity. People who live there have their own luxury homes on the base, and when they go offsite to visit relatives they are apparently taped 24/7 and are forbidden to discuss matters about the base.

Several ex-employees describe common experiences – working alongside other-worldly beings called the greys. Telekinetic dimensional beings. Many ex-employees have pictures of UFO craft and say the pilots are non-human – one or two feet tall.

It has been claimed that the Roswell Crash in 1947 was not a crash at all – the USAF was given permission to shoot an alien craft down. The official line is that it was a weather balloon project and the wreckage was simply that. To understand this story better, you have to be aware of project Mogul.

Project Mogul (sometimes referred to as Operation Mogul) was a top secret project by the US Army and Air Force involving microphones flown on high-altitude balloons, whose primary purpose was long-distance detection of sound waves generated by Soviet atomic bomb tests. The project was carried out from 1947 until early 1949. The project was moderately successful, but was very expensive and was superseded by a network of seismic detectors and air sampling for fallout, which were cheaper, more reliable, and easier to deploy and operate.

When this top secret balloon equipment crashed, the forces were quick to recover the classified equipment, for feat of letting the public know what the project was really designed to monitor – Russian nuclear tests. Later that day, the press reported that a weather balloon was recovered by the RAAF personnel. A press conference was held, featuring debris (foil, rubber and wood) said to be from the crashed object, which matched the weather balloon description. Historian Robert Goldberg wrote that the intended effect was achieved, and "the story died the next day".

The first conspiracy book about Roswell was The Roswell Incident (1980) by Charles Berlitz and William Moore. The book may very well have sparked the entire alien connection, claiming that a spacecraft was hit by lightning and crashed at Roswell, killing the alien pilots. The book also claimed that all materials were confiscated by the authorities and were replaced by weather balloon wreckage – the press were not allowed to inspect anything. Here also was the first mention of eye-witnesses spotting alien corpses in the crash site.

Subsequent investigations say only seven people actually saw the wreckage first hand, and only five of them handled the remains. It concluded that the rest of the stories and details were a combination of sensationalism, hoaxes, fuzzy memories and embellishment. The party line is that Roswell has been thoroughly investigated and totally debunked. Yet it remains a curious and fascinating event, and it's been great for the movie industry, tourism and the town of Roswell itself.

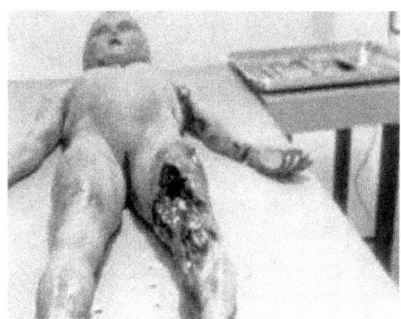

In 1995, film footage purporting to show an alien autopsy and claimed to have been taken by a US military official shortly after the Roswell incident was released by Ray Santilli, a London-based video entrepreneur. The footage caused an international sensation when it aired on television networks around the world. In 2006, Santilli said that the film was mostly a reconstruction, but continued to claim it was based on genuine footage now lost, and some original frames that had supposedly survived. A fictionalized version of the creation of the footage and its release was retold in the comedy film Alien Autopsy in 2006.

In another bizarre twist, American journalist Annie Jacobsen's "Area 51: An Uncensored History of America's Top Secret Military Base" published in 2011, based on interviews with scientists and engineers who worked in Area 51, dismisses the alien story. She quotes one unnamed source as claiming that Josef Mengele, a German Schutzstaffel officer and a physician in Auschwitz, was recruited by the Soviet leader Joseph Stalin to produce "grotesque, child-size aviators" to be remotely piloted and landed in America in order to cause hysteria similar to Orson Welles' War of the Worlds (1938). The aircraft, however, crashed and the incident was hushed up by the Americans. Jacobsen wrote that the bodies found at the crash site were children around 12 years old with large heads and abnormally-shaped, over-sized eyes. They were neither aliens nor consenting airmen, but human guinea pigs. The book was criticized for extensive errors by scientists from the Federation of American Scientists.

During World War 2 it is suggested that anti-gravity technology was being developed by the Nazis? To this day there are strange platforms and rigs built during the 1940's which defy explanation. In operation paperclip the German scientists moved to the USA and it is perfectly feasible that they continued to develop this technology at Area 51.

After Roswell lots of alien UFO sightings were reported and other incidents. Then again, you must remember that this was a time period when they had just been through two world wars, they were obsessed with the atom bomb, reds under the bed, the dangers of radiation, the space race, a time period full of fear, technology, the future.

Many of the UFO sightings were explained away as civilians seeing the U2 spy plane in operation.

The mainstream explanation is that this is indeed a top secret military base in the USA. You can't fly over it, you often see photographers watching from afar with telescopic lenses. We know that the military have secret project and classified matters. We should leave them alone and let them do their secret stuff.

I've heard a recording of a private plane pilot who flies onto the restricted airspace over Area 51. In the audio you can hear him narrating what he sees, and then you hear the Air Force jets hailing him and demanding that he leaves the restricted airspace. When he refuses, you hear the muffled sounds of an explosion or a crash. It seems the Air Force shot a civilian aircraft down.

There are multitudes of alien sightings and UFO incidents, but the Roswell incident is what sparked people's interest in Area 51 originally.

Weapons Of Mass Distraction

Just suppose there's a global power elite - a superclass – history is full of secret societies who were manipulating events and plotting to create their idealised world view and a global central bank. Using mass surveillance, propaganda and state terrorism they aim to put a dictatorial leader on a pedestal, built up by a cult of personality, and then convince us that they will lead us all to their greater end goal.

Mass surveillance. CCTV. Mobile GPS tracking. Your phone line and text messages can be hacked. Credit card transactions are recorded and tracked. All Point of sale transactions get recorded, then the next day your mailbox is full of related offers. You can look at hotels on Google for a holiday in Orlando, and then you go to Facebook and up come adverts for hotels in Orlando. This is called "retargeting". Even Disney scans your fingerprint in order to enter the parks. Big Brother is indeed watching you.

Human population control. Health & Family planning programmes. Fluoridation was used by the Nazis. Now it's in our water, AND our toothpaste. Maybe even mouthwash as well. Genetically Modified Food. Mass vaccinations. Genocide, unnecessary wars, plagues, engineered viruses [Ebola], engineering the weather [using chemtrails, tsunamis, earthquakes]. The Defense Advanced Research Projects Agency (DARPA) is an agency of the U.S. Department of Defense responsible for the development of emerging technologies for use by the military. They have been developing technologies since 1958. Their information awareness office featured an all seeing eye looking over the globe. There's that all-seeing eye symbol again. Look at AOL's brand. Look at CBS News logo. The antichrist is blind in one eye. It's even on the back of the one dollar bill.

Then there's the mind control aspect. Imagine how the mass media could be used to manufacture a culture of fear and a national consensus. Mistrusting and mutually fearing population are much easier to influence. The aim would be to subvert your thinking and your own behaviours and decisions by using projects like MK Ultra and subliminal advertising – both existed and both worked very, very well]

That brings us to the aliens and UFO's. Are they aliens or are they demonic entities? Reported to answer you in your mind in your own voice. Could they be not from other worlds, but other dimensions? We used to think there were three dimensions. String theory from Quantum Physics now says there are 36. Could aliens actually be fallen angel hybrids?

After the Roswell UFO incident, Majestic 12 was supposed to have been formed in 1947 by President Harry S. Truman - formed as a covert US government organisation that allegedly collaborated with aliens. They offered the 'beings' a deal - trade human abduction and experimentation in return for technology and biotech. Most of which is housed and developed to this day in Area 51. Yet all the while they are studying us...

Also worth noting is The New Age movement – over the last 50 years we've witnessed a growth in alternative medicine, astrology, quantum mysticism. All of these ideologies have been growing in popularity, while faith in the establishment and religion is plummeting. Hypnosis, visualisation, tarot, meditation, spiritual healing can all be studied in the "pop psychology" section of any good bookstore. Yet 200 years ago you would have been burned at the stake like a witch for practicing any of them...

Then there's the supernatural and magic. Two hundred years ago people were burned at the stake for being a witch. But thanks to Harry Potter and Walt Disney, spellcasting, talismans, amulets and voodoo curses are mainstream, even child friendly! I saw an advert for a kids zombie toy the other day. Here you go little Amy, go and play with your little friend – one of the carnivorous living dead.

What Should I Be Looking For?

There are blatant clues everywhere you look. The Simpsons famously predicted 911. In the X-men cartoon in the 80's it shows people being microchipped. Your money is on the chip. Comply or they wipe the chip. You will all bow down to the NOW, or else. And this is a kid's show!

The right to bear arms is part of the American constitution. There have been a number of shooting spree incidents in the USA [Sandy Hook for example] where some "unstable" individual takes a firearm and kills dozens of innocent children, youths and citizens. They are then tried and convicted as we watch eye-witness reports and empathise with the traumatised community. Then new gun laws are passed in that State to take the ownership of domestic firearms away from the general public. One suggestion is that the general population are gradually being disarmed, while the authorities stockpile weaponised drones, artificially intelligent robots and large amounts of live ammunition.

What if these shooting incidents and others like the Boston marathon and missing Indonesian planes are simply "false flags" – media engineered smokescreens to distract and occupy the masses and misdirect their attention from what is really going on?

Isn't it feasible that the NWO could create incidents involving firearms, create a mass panic, so laws can be passed to protect us all, and take the arms away? Meanwhile the Doomsday preppers are reinforcing their basements, stockpiling food, and arming themselves for the oncoming apocalypse. The rich have designer bunkers in vast underground complexes. It would be child's play for the Federal Reserve to cause a financial collapse in the economy.

This concept has grown by the decade. Radical right wing gun culture is growing. The X-Files TV series made conspiracies and UFO's completely acceptable to the masses. The 2008 financial crisis was predicted by economists five years earlier, yet it was still permitted to happen. You should ask yourself why?

On one side we have Fox News which has been continually criticised for supporting the New World Order's doctrines. The media portray the major politicians as enemies but actually they are all allies Frosty relationship between Tony Blair and Angela Markel is just a performance for the population. Putin was in the KGB and meets regularly with Obama. Obama might be a Muslim.

On the other hand we have radio host Alex Jones, who created Infowars.com to highlight the big picture and oppose the NWO. Jesse Ventura and a wealth of other websites trying to wake people up.

Which will you be watching tomorrow?

What If It's True?

Here's the mainstream argument: each of our respective country's government is doing the best they can with the resources they have, they meet at Camp David and other large conferences, laws are passed, we can trust their judgement and leadership because we have a vote and we decide who's in power, and everything is going to be alright. Be a good citizen, pay your taxes and all will be well 🙂

SCEPTICS would say that people mistrust the government, so we should stand up and rebel. The conspiracists are linking unconnected myths and events to try and fabricate a back story to explain It all. Crackpot theories from sad individuals who can't take things at face value.

They would say that the reason you're scared and worried about a new world order, is that you have a strong viewpoint, but no power to change the system, you care deeply about freedom of choice yet you feel powerless in your own life. Psychologists call that "agency panic", and that weakness causes you to rebel against authority and claim that everyone is out to manipulate you.

We're entering the new Age of Aquarius according to western astrology. At the time of writing there have been 4 blood red moons in the sky – there's a fifth one in September 2015, which is supposed to be a biblical event.

Pope Francis says it's alright to believe in evolution, UFO's. You don't have to believe in God.

Pope Francis will visit the White house for the first time – perhaps all hell will break loose?

By the time you read this, we'll know already...

Why should you care either way?

Well, the implication is that the Americans have not only encountered extra-terrestrial beings, they have formed an alliance and have worked together for over fifty years, studying the spacecraft and its technology, and they've used that technology. The greys and US military are allies, and the USAF have superior craft, weapon and technology. That means weapons that could wipe the human race out. That could include biotech that could eradicate disease. A cure for cancer?

Now if this were true, shouldn't the general public know about it? Doesn't that then beg the question why are we still being ravaged by diseases like Cancer and HIV when there may be a solution? Or is it as simple as the big pharmaceutical companies make money by keeping the masses ill and on their regular medication, which is of course a highly consumed, repeat purchase.

Perhaps the Royal family lives as long as they have because of the biomedical technology the elite have access to, including cures for diseases. Look carefully at photographs of the Royals emerging from hospitals. The nurse's uniforms are clearly adorned with Freemason symbolism. The rich and powerful have been promised longer lives and sustained health. Note that Obama and Putin don't drink the bottled water at events. They must have their own supply...

Allegedly the deal was that the aliens can study us and harvest our DNA, in return for access to their technology. That would explain all the reported crop circles, cattle mutilations, and the multitudes of alien abduction cases.

The frightening aspect is that the general public is being kept in the dark, IF we have cures for things that are ravaging the planet, but there's no money in cures so we'll never get access to them. Remember that the world's richest families run the planet. The Illuminati control the resources and the media. Some people believe that the New World Order will let the greys take over, as they are a superior race with advanced technology and far more developed intellects. On one video I have seen what looks like a 7' tall grey being killing a man using telekinesis. Perhaps there are even human/alien hybrids.

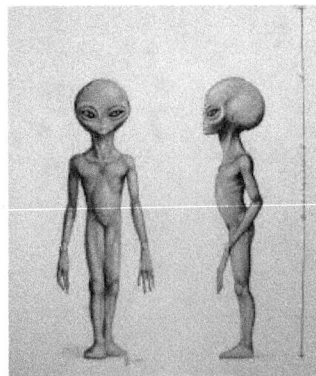

The nightmare scenario is that there is an alliance with the aliens who could easily invade or decimate the human race, or perhaps enslave us.

Perhaps the aliens are not what they claim to be. Perhaps they are actually angels and demons, and not aliens. Most cultures on the planet have legends and myths about little people with magic powers: leprechauns, fairies. Smarter than us, who have abilities that we don't have, always secretive. Or the recurring tales of Incubi and Succubi – male and female entities paralysing the human as they lie in their bed. Could they be aliens, or are they another species - maybe in another dimension that we can't perceive?

Near death experience [NDE] survivors talk about the spirit world, and there is no hell. Some people use Ouija boards and try to conjure up the spirits of the dead. Perhaps we are not contacting the dead; perhaps we are contacting this other race?

Material that is classified eventually gets declassified. It was revealed in the last few years that a British troop ship sank in World War Two and hundreds of British soldiers drowned at sea, and Churchill wanted this disaster covered up. So it was.

Do you think that maybe in fifty years we will learn what really happened on September 11th? Will we eventually learn what happened to the missing Malaysian jet MH370? Or are these simply acts of misdirection to keep your eyes off the important machinations...

Repeated School killings with teenagers firing guns. Madeleine McCann. The heart breaking story of a child going missing, two parents leaving their child unattended in a foreign hotel to go to a bar. Never mind the issues of parental responsibility. We keep seeing picture in the media of how she would look now. Very often the public is fed tantalising titbits to keep them preoccupied...

What do YOU believe, dear reader? It's often said that ordinary people have small libraries and big televisions, but extraordinary people have big libraries and small televisions, or no television. We live in a world where practically every house has a 402 or bigger television, and it talks pride of place on a wall somewhere for the occupants to stare at endlessly. I once heard it called "The electronic income reducer". It doesn't make you money. In fact it costs you electricity and licences. Just think about it. The average American spends 5 hours a day watching TV.

As I work on this book there is stuff happening in our world. The media has a direct influence on what we do day to day. The question is, it all pre-scripted and written to control the general masses? Or is it fair and objective reporting by honest and careful journalists who value truth and fact over money and ratings?

CNN news reporters have come forward to say they are regularly paid to tell fabricated lies. Another name for your TV is "The tell lie vision". These stories break on every news channel at the same time. You see pictures of shooting scenes like Sandy Hook or Columbine. In the media we see pictures of a foreign journalist interviewing a witness with dead bodies behind them. Careful scrutiny later shows the same people in a different country in a different incident, but with the exact same images.

With the Sandy Hook school shooting incident – there exists dash cam footage at the exact time the incident showing a normal, empty car park. A Facebook page to support the victims, only it was set up the day BEFORE the shooting. There's been a host of accusations that some of the parents in one event are the same parents as were at the Boston marathon bombing. In fact I know someone who was at the Boston marathon, and insist that she saw fake blood capsules, and an amputee being wheeled away. Any paramedic will tell you that the last thing you do with someone who's lost a leg is pick them up and sit them on a wheelchair!

So there you have it. The New World order are headed by the elite rich and run the government, and the military. The US government may have encountered aliens and developed advanced technology as a result. At the very least. Possibly much worse than that. What if all the Spielberg movies and Hollywood blockbusters have been slowly conditioning the public into the idea that aliens might exist. How do you tell your kids what's coming? Or do you let George Lucas and J.J. Abrams do that for you?

FACT: The zombie movie "World War Z" has an opening sequence which was shot nor far from where I live in Glasgow. It features a scene where a garbage lorry goes out of control in George Square, mowing several people in the crowd down before crashing to a halt. The movie was released in 2013. In Glasgow on Christmas 2014 a garbage lorry went out of control in Glasgow's George Square killing six people in the crowd before crashing to a halt. Coincidence? Could be.

I can envisage how the global agenda will gradually roll out. Perhaps weapons of mass destruction, or an alien virus that could wipe us out in droves. The richest families could hide underground in luxury bunkers and only re-emerge when it's safe to do so.

How else do you explain the scores of first hand reports of alien abductions and close encounters? Abductees have found bits of metal in their body, metal that science can't identify. Some have marks on their body. Some report seeing hybrid children with big eyes. Is this all just post-traumatic stress, or delusional hallucinations? That wouldn't explain the metal fragments in their body...

The RAF have reported ufo's, and dozens of airline pilots too. It appears there is SOMETHING flying around up there, and it's not us.

At the time of writing there have been numerous reports of a social media terrorist groom by ISIS to teach several people how to build a bomb in 5 cities across the UK, using a pressure cooker for the device. Now one of my business colleagues was a bomb disposal man in the army and a lot of his contacts have told him not to be in the city centre this weekend. If your mobile phone goes dead then you're in the danger zone. They deactivate mobile phone masts to prevent them being used to trigger a bomb.

Also at the time of writing NASA have declared there is flowing water on Mars. And where there is water, there is usually life...

And have you ever noticed that the social media bomber would be reported in the news headlines BEFORE the water on Mars item. Why is that? What's the order of priority?

So is Area 51 a dangerous idea? A top secret haven of alien biotech and unspeakable weapons of mass distraction? Or is it simply a classified military base surrounded by a series of myths that are more like weapons of mass distraction? You decide what you want to believe.

Get The Next Dangerous Idea...

This is only one of the NINE dangerous ideas I have written about. Each of these is guaranteed to create a debate in the pub or over the dinner table. The Illuminati, 911, and The Moon Landings are amongst the others. To register for our VIP reader list and get updates on all the latest releases, just register at www.9DangerousIdeas.com

Copyright and Disclaimer

About The Author

If you're like me, you probably feel like we're being denied the truth, leaving us to be the working cattle that keep society ticking over, right?

And you probably believe that the powers that be deliberately engineer world changing events for their own power and gain, costing us our freedom, health and civil rights... yes?

The truth is you have no idea how to change it or beat the puppet masters. If you did then you'd be doing it.

Your aim is probably to determine the facts and uncover the truth, wake up more people and let them make up their own minds. Because deep down you truly value your freedom and having a bright future for your kids

But you're absolutely terrified that some sceptic will pick holes in your argument and you'll have nothing to answer with'

Doesn't it frustrate you when friends and family don't believe you, you're not taken seriously, or worse - you're being thought of as a crackpot? You know that the agenda is being pushed forward through the mainstream media but you haven't figured out what to do about it yet...

And you know deep down that if you could just raise their awareness, wake people up, and get them to stand up for what we believe in...

And you'd probably jump for joy if you could convince more people to look into conspiracy theories and question authority.

But you've tried showing them the explosion of web sites, blogs and videos before and tried to convince other people that you're right, or that they should at least look into it, yet you still have very little buy-in

I know how you feel - you've always wanted to get people to listen to you, and get them to see that they're being lied to and they're not really free. But there's a nagging doubt inside that wonders if you know enough about conspiracy theories to be taken seriously?

So you surf the web looking for moon landing hoaxes, conspiracy theories and Freemasons - or you keep up to date with David Icke, Alex Jones and Infowars.com. But don't you just hate it when you have to argue with friends, family and colleagues who don't believe you?!

How much more money do you have to spend on books and DVDs before the penny drops?

I always thought "if only someone could show them a fair summary of both sides of the argument so they can make up their own mind"... Then I realise that yet again, I forgot to get all my facts straight before jumping into the next debate...

I grew up a good catholic boy, loving space stuff – I had my own telescope, loved sci-fi, the space shuttle. But have you ever noticed that all the big events happen in or are connected to The United States of America? Being outside the USA we can see it more objectively, as we're not subjected to the same level of conditioning and patriotism. Some call it brainwashing. I used to discuss the moon landings with my Dad, and he didn't believe the official line. He told me to research it for myself so I did. That sparked the usual questions - why were there no visible stars in the sky above the moon, why was the flag waving, why were there astronaut footprints but no tyre tracks from the moon rover ?

In 2001 I was still at primary school when 911 happened– and I didn't buy it. I was at a relative's house when the two towers were shown on the news. Too many questionable factors. The 16th Century philosopher Nostradamus was rumoured to have predicted two Everyone else bought into the Bin Laden explanation but my uncle and I didn't buy it. We discussed it amongst ourselves and felt almost guilty for questioning it. Those buildings looked like they were brought down by controlled demolition. The BBC newscaster who reported the destruction of Building 7... BEFORE the building fell. And if a plane really did hit the Pentagon, why was all the CCTV footage confiscated? So I started looking into it on YouTube, and other internet sites, where I watched videos about Bohemian Grove with all the world's leaders present. Then I realised the implications of it all...

There's a guy in my street who is a Mason. I was always curious about the secret society that was allegedly started by the Vatican. Pope John Paul was shot in 1981 and there was a story about him throwing up a Freemason symbol for help. When I broached the subject with my neighbour he was taken aback at first, but then got quite excited at my curiosity...

Hollywood actors and celebrities displaying esoteric symbols and performing symbolic rituals on stage. Disney friendly Hannah Montana turning into twerking Miley Cyrus. Britney going from sassy schoolgirl to skinhead meltdown. Hollywood celebrities and powerful people who start to speak out and then die under mysterious circumstances. Michael Jackson. Whitney Houston. Paul Walker

Have you ever seen weird lights in the sky? I have... in the skies above Scotland. Three years ago I saw a red orb in the sky at night while out with a mate, which moved in a strange way for a good five minutes. We were so scared, we couldn't tell what it was. So we agreed to keep that to ourselves and we never talked about it. There have been far too many abductions, crop circles and mutilated cattle cases to ignore.

I've been to places where Satanists have carved the trees and sacrificed small animals. I've also been arrested for breach of the peace, and had the Police at my door.

But I never found anyone to really discuss it with. My friends thought I was bonkers. It DOES sound crazy - that the mainstream media is controlled and feeds the public only certain info – enough to keep them preoccupied and distracted while the real agenda rolls on. Think about bird flu, the Ebola outbreak. While we were distracted by them, what was really going on?

Rather than being some evangelistic preacher who tries to convince you, I want to give you both sides of the argument and let you make an informed decision. There's no going back. You can't ignore the signs, there are too many inconsistencies. I have spoken at length to an old friend who started off certain that the moon landings happened as reported, but now he's changed his mind. My goal now is to share these alleged conspiracies with other people and let them decide themselves. Stand up and be counted. We can bring them down. The 85% majority can topple the world elite. The truth is out there...